Chosen
and
Changed

Breaking Generational Brokenness
for the Glory of God

Chosen and Changed

Breaking Generational Brokenness for the Glory of God

Robbin L. Reid

TJS PUBLISHING HOUSE

Published in the United States of America

First Printing, 2024

ISBN-13: 978-1-952833-65-6
ISBN-10: 1-952833-65-5
Cover design by TJS Publishing House

Published by TJS Publishing House
www.tjspublishinghouse.com
contact@tjspublishinghouse.com

DEDICATION

All the Glory Belongs to God!

Brian and Britne,

I dedicate this book to you. You have changed my life from day one. You're both very valuable to me. From the moment you both arrived, I knew my life was no longer going to be only about me, and just your existence made me strive to do better. Without the both of you, I don't know where I would be. Not only did you open my heart, but you opened my eyes and my ears. Not only do I dedicate this book to the two of you, but also to my sweet Aubree and the flock of all my grandchildren from every generation to come.

Brian, you are my firstborn. Thank you for being patient with me and waiting for me to grow up as a first-time mother. As you read this book, you will see I really did my best. I am very proud of you and your gentle heart. Know that you have the ability in you *right now* to become all God desires for your life journey. I admire your strength, perseverance, and your determination to press ahead during difficult times. Always be present for my grandchildren, emotionally and financially. Most importantly, be a man of your word.

Britne, you're everything I always wanted to be. I intentionally sacrificed my life, time, and energy for you. I poured into you and gave all I had. I am so proud of the young lady you're becoming. I love your determination and excellence in everything you do. Your discipline and achievements. A woman of all trades and a master of all. Don't forget, you're the grand prize.

The generational blessings continue with you two. As you read this book, I want you to measure the generations from now to the future generations. You both have God-given purpose and gifts on this earth to fix problems, and you have the responsibility to be a great example for the next generation.

> But seek ye first the kingdom of God, and his righteousness and all these things shall be added unto you. (Matthew 6:33 KJV)

Build your success on what Christ says. Chase after Christ and the things of the kingdom, not worldly possessions, and everything will be added unto you.

I love you to life,

Mom

CONTENTS

FOREWORD

Throughout my life, my mom has been my strong, determined, loving, God-Fearing role model. Her strength and perseverance were sculpted through the hardships she faced as a child. Growing up with a mother who struggled to provide the love and stability she longed for made her break the generational curse full of women who were broken, uneducated, mishandled, rejected, and poor. Instead of allowing the past to define who she is, she made her own decision and mission to raise me in a warm and nurturing environment, the one she longed for.

Every single day, she instilled in me the values of compassion, perseverance, and confidence. Through her guidance, I've learned to confront life's challenges with courage. No matter the struggles she faced, whether it was emotional or financial, she approached each challenge with grace. Her ability to find strength in God motivates me that no matter the circumstance, I can get through any and everything with Yahweh.

Mom has taught me that setbacks are just setups for comebacks. Her commitment to my happiness and success shows the unconditional love she has in her heart for me. Each venting session, when I just didn't know what to do, every encouragement during my struggles, through all the times I wanted to give up, and the countless sacrifices she made even when she didn't have it at the moment, all have helped me and gotten me through hard times. I am endlessly grateful for her influence, and I cherish the bond we share.

As I look back, I realize that her strength is not just the absence of struggle but the victory that blossoms from it. I love her for all that she does, and I hope to honor her legacy by living a life filled with love and resilience, just as she always wanted for me.

Love, your beautiful daughter,

Britne

PROLOGUE

"Before I formed you in the womb I knew you; Before you were born I sanctified you; I ordained you a prophet to the nations." (Jeremiah 1:5 NKJV)

I wrote this book to encourage you, to empower you, and to let you know how God has changed my life. Even through my trials and struggles, He was always there.

There is purpose in my pain. He took the trauma and adversities of my life from just barely surviving into surrendering to His perfect will, which led to hope. Hope turned into strength, and strength turned into determination. Determination turned into perseverance and courage. Then, I entered into his unmerited grace and favor. His favor led me boldly into victory. It's not where you start, but it's how you finish!

"'For I know the plans I have for you,' declares the Lord, 'plans to prosper you and not to harm you, plans to give you hope and a future.'" (Jeremiah 29:11 NIV)

I've often asked myself why God chose me to come to this place called Life to live in poverty and such poor conditions. *What significance did I have?* I have always felt like I was the "black sheep" everywhere I went. I was so different. I looked differently, talked differently, and thought differently. I was talked about, teased, and rejected by others, including my family. I walked around for decades unsure of my purpose. I often thought, *Surely, God has made a mistake.*

Please allow me to take you on my journey, to show you why I felt like an outcast, out of place and lacking purpose. That is, until the day God revealed my purpose. In spite of my own doubts and initial hesitancy, God equipped me and provided me with all I needed to walk in His purpose. He allowed me to influence lives and break generational curses, providing love and nurturing to the most innocent of His children.

CHAPTER 1

Foundation Park
Before I Was Conceived in My Mother's Womb

My mother came from generations of women who were mishandled, rejected, abused, broken, uneducated, and poor. Early age pregnancy, dropping out of school, and abusive relationships abounded. Alcohol abuse, partying, surviving on welfare and government assistance were standard. Barely getting by in low-income housing while battling low self-esteem and believing they had no value in life had become normalized. This way of life haunted several generations of women long before my mother was even born, and she sustained the pattern. As the oldest of what would be my mother's six children, I unknowingly continued the legacy.

My mother conceived me at the age of fourteen. A baby having a baby. Both of my parents were very young at the time. It was one of those typical adolescent "flings" that wasn't going to last, but during the relationship came a surprise . . . guess who? Me!

I was born at Norfolk Community Hospital in Virginia in December of 1969, just before Christmas, into a world I can only describe as *a hot mess*. My childhood was scary, a consistent cold, dark feeling. We were the definition of what would be in today's terminology *food insecure*. I lived in a space of being constantly hungry, which is to say, I lived in a space of fear. Always. My go-to meal was to ask my mother for a slice of bread and some water, reminiscent of solitary confinement in a prison cell or military brig. My gourmet meal was a peanut butter and jelly sandwich with dry macaroni pasta.

My biological father was drafted into the Army before I was born, and soon after, my mother married another man. We lived in low-income project housing called Foundation Park off of Shelton Road in Chesapeake, Virginia. The houses were old, white, former military housing, that should have been condemned, but were instead being used for low-income families. To add insult to injury, rats would come into my bedroom, their long tails waving as they sniffed and scurried in search of nonexistent food scraps. I was too scared to call for help. The danger on the other side of my bedroom wall was more frightening than the rats.

A short time later, my mother gave birth to her second child, my brother. As a young child of only three years old, I remember hearing my stepdad yelling at my mother, but his booming voice was still not as loud as her screams for help. I heard it all. The shattering of thrown glass. Him smacking her in the face and throwing her against walls. Punching and stomping her, over and over and over, as she screamed out, "Stop!" over and over and over.

My mother would cry out in vain for help. I couldn't help her, young as I was, because I was scared he would do the same to me. Instead, I lay in bed with my little brother next to me in the dark, terrified, holding on to him as protection, even though I was the oldest.

My stepdad would repeatedly abuse my mother. It seemed to me they fought every day. Back then, I didn't know why, although later, it was revealed to me he was a very jealous person. I would hear screaming and, oftentimes, the commotion would wake me out of my sleep. Curiosity would get the best of me, and if I could steal a glance of the aftermath, I would witness blood running down my mother's face and lips. It was a sad existence for all of us, and I learned it was better to not come out of my room, regardless of how loud the violence became. Sometimes, most times, he would beat her up, and afterward they would have sex; and sometimes, they would have sex first, and then he would beat her up. I could hear all of this from my room. I would routinely pee on myself because I was afraid to get up out of the bed, fearing I would suffer the same fate.

Abusing anyone to control them is wrong. Parents and guardians need to realize how their abusive relationships can have a lasting effect on children's self-worth. My mother's abusive relationship was my first encounter with fear and neglect because it was a continuous cycle. It has also affected my decisions from childhood and even now in adulthood. Parents need to understand that their children are aware of the violence and very much affected by it, even when it appears otherwise.

If you or someone you know is in an abusive relationship, carefully seek help. The National Domestic Violence Hotline can be reached at 1-800-799-7233, or you can text 88788 for assistance.

Back in those days, it seemed that succumbing to violence as a woman was the only option. My grandmother and aunts were being abused by their husbands. My uncles were abusing their girlfriends and wives, like that was what was necessary to do, a need to control them. I remember the house lights got turned off for not paying the bill, and my stepdad and mom fought in the dark, with a candle in a mason jar flickering in the corner.

It is something to hear your mother cry for help in agony. Indescribable. She suffered in pain, relentlessly crying for help as my stepdad beat her. I was so scared, so powerless to help. But I can never remember a time when she fought back.

My mother was beautiful. *Why would anyone want to hurt her?* People called her red-bone because she was light-skinned. Her fair complexion revealed her daily trauma, and it was normal for me to see her bruised up with black eyes.

I loved my mother, but I didn't think she loved me because I *never* heard those words come out of her mouth. But I remember asking her if I could walk to the store with her, and she said yes. I was *so* happy! So happy that I walked to the store barefoot on unpaved roads, listening to her say, "Watch out for all the glass!" I thought, *she must care if she is concerned about me getting glass in my foot.*

The cycle of abuse continued. I don't know if my stepdad put us out, or if my mother got fed up with the abuse and found the courage to leave. But we finally left.

"Even to your old age and gray hairs
   I am he, I am he who will sustain you.
I have made you and I will carry you;
   I will sustain you and I will rescue you."

Isaiah 46:4 NIV

I realize that my birthday was the devil's death-day. I had to go through my family's generational journey to purposefully see my own journey. God is faithful.

Father, I pray for your protection no matter where I am. I will look to you as my protector, the one who fights for me every day. You are my hiding place and under your wings I can always find shelter from danger and trouble. Thank you for the hideout.

In Jesus' name, Amen!

CHAPTER 2

Queen City, Virginia: The Outhouse

My father was still in the Vietnam War, while we were in a war of our own. My mother separated from her husband, and we moved in with her parents, my grandparents, and those living conditions were even worse. Eleven people were living in a two-bedroom house. This was truly "the house that Jack built." More a frame than a house, with not much inside of it. It was a gray, two-story structure that leaned. There was no indoor plumbing, no running water in the house. Whenever we needed to use the bathroom during the day, we had to go to the outhouse, and we used old newspapers as toilet tissue. At night, we brought a five-gallon bucket into the house to use as our toilet, and in the morning, we would go outside and dump it into a ditch, rinse out the bucket, and hang it outside on the clothesline to air dry.

Since we didn't have any running water, we used a water pump located outside in the yard. We pumped however much water we needed into a pail and then brought it inside the house to boil it first, getting the "rust" out of the water before using it. Since we didn't have a toilet, bathroom sink, tub, shower, or any sort of indoor plumbing, we would use the pumped water from the well to take baths using a hospital wash pan.

We did have electricity, but only in one room downstairs in the kitchen. We ran extension cords through the kitchen to the other rooms downstairs. There were no electrical lights upstairs and it was pitch black, save scarce light from the moon shining in a window. We had to walk up the stairs slowly, holding on to the walls as a guide so we wouldn't trip. No window fans or air conditioning. No central heat, just a wood stove and a kerosene heater. My granddaddy would chop down trees with an axe, and then my brothers would stack the wood on the back porch to use as firewood. To make the fire inside the house, we had to fill the wood stove with tree bark, add kerosene, and then light some newspaper to get the fire going before closing the door to the stove. The upstairs was heated by the warmth of the chimney that went up the interior of the home. But once the fire went out, the upstairs areas were freezing! There was no insulation throughout the whole house, and we could literally see outside through the cracks in the boards.

Although we had a gas stove to cook on, there was no running water to wash the dishes. That water, too, had to be hand-pumped and brought in from the water pump outside.

We didn't have a refrigerator. We used a Styrofoam cooler to store milk, eggs, cheese, and anything else that needed to be refrigerated. Sometimes, the house was so cold that my grandmother would simply place the milk on the windowsill. Later on, we did get an actual refrigerator.

The house was infested with roaches, mice, and rats. There was even a rooster that ran around outside with the cats and the dogs. The living conditions were horrible. We couldn't ever actually bathe, so we would take "wash-ups" in the hospital wash pan once a week on Sundays. We wore the same clothes for a whole week. Most of my siblings shared two bunk beds, and by this time, there were six of us. If someone peed in the bed, we all went to school smelling like urine unless we could find something else to wear. But we couldn't wash our actual bodies until Sunday. That would be wasting water.

I remember going to school smelling like urine, with my hair knotty and my belly always hungry. The house was so infested that our food boxes had droppings of rat feces on them. Because of the outhouse, there was a swarm of flies every day. Roaches climbed all over the walls. At night, we wrapped ourselves tightly in our quilt, not only to keep warm, but to keep the roaches from climbing all over us, fearing they might get into our ears.

We washed our clothes once a week in a wash tub using a washboard. We used Ivory bar soap to wash our dishes, clothes, and body. Sometimes, if we managed to acquire laundry detergent, we used it to wash our dishes, clothes, and body. We were so dirty that when our uncle came over, he would bathe us in the wash tub we used to wash the laundry, and he would use Ajax toilet cleaner and SOS pads on our skin to scour off the dirt. My skin was so sore, especially around my neck and back, from him scrubbing so hard, especially if he was angry.

Living in that house was hell. There was definitely a dark cloud of hatred hanging over us, no love. I walked barefoot most of my childhood because I had to save my shoes for school. I was not allowed to bring home schoolbooks because my granddaddy, "Doc," said he was not paying for any books that got lost. When Doc would come home, my siblings and I would take turns taking off his boots and fanning him with a record album until he fell asleep. If we made too much noise and woke him up, we would get a beating. If we laughed too much or too loud, we would get a beating. We were beaten with a switch or a belt, sometimes both.

Living in that house was like living in a prison. There was no respect for children. We were to be seen, but not heard. The living conditions we endured were seemingly by choice because the neighbors all around us lived in nicer homes with indoor plumbing and all the conveniences of modern-day living during that time. They even had window air conditioning. We only had a box fan in our window, hoping a cool breeze would come through.

I really felt like this was a choice my mother made, from bad to worse, and I often asked, *God, where are you? I know you didn't choose me for this, to live this type of lifestyle.*

God says in I Corinthians 10:13 NIV, "No temptation has overtaken you except what is common to mankind". And God is faithful; he will not let you be tempted beyond what you can bear. But when you are tempted, he will also provide a way out so that you can endure it."

I cannot emphasize it enough. My mother had us living in filth. No running water, no plumbing, no toilet, no sink, no bathtub, no electricity, no air conditioning, a wood stove and a kerosene heater for heat. No insulation in the house. As innocent children, our bodies were dingy, mangy, and smelly. We were hot and we were cold. We were incessantly hungry. Maggots, flies, roaches, mice, and rats were pervasive. Chickens, cats, and dogs ran aimlessly around in the yard. *We are living like slaves!* I thought.

One would think we lived in the country, but *nope!* Smack dab in the city in the middle of Virginia Beach in a black neighborhood called Queen City, acquiring its name because so many beautiful women lived in the area that the residents adopted the moniker. The neighborhood is actually one of over a dozen historically black neighborhoods featured in a 72-page historical research paper from 2017, entitled History of African American Communities in Princess Anne County/Virginia Beach. If anyone drove through Queen City now, they would be amazed at the changes. Paved streets, city water, and sewer. Most improvements not made until the late 1990s.

The Bible says in Proverbs 23:7 KJV, "For as he thinketh in his heart, so is he. . ." There was something in me, in my thoughts, in my imaginings, that saw better for my life!

CHAPTER 3

Four Years Old

My mother always had a 'man.' That was one thing she never had to worry about. She would take care of her 'man' before she would take care of her children. We were hungry, but her 'man' ate very well.

My mother started disappearing from my life. She would be gone for days and days at a time. Because I would cry if I knew she was leaving, she would sneak out of the house, saying she was going to the corner store to get cigarettes, promising she would be right back. But she would be gone for days, sometimes weeks. She wouldn't leave with extra clothes, so I always took her at her word that she would be right back. She left us with my grandparents, and because she did, out of anger and frustration, they would beat us.

My grandfather was very abusive toward my grandmother. I think that's why my grandmother became an alcoholic, that, and she knew my mother was involved in an incestuous relationship with my granddaddy, my mother's stepfather. I am not sure why or at what age my mother started drinking alcohol, but she also ended up being an alcoholic.

When my uncle came over, he, too, would beat us for no reason, mostly because we simply weren't moving fast enough. My uncle and grandmother would gossip about my mother leaving us at home to go sleep with a man while leaving us with no food to eat.

One day, a family friend was braiding my hair, and my uncle called my name. I didn't jump right up to see what he wanted (which was the expectation for children) because she was in the middle of a braid. In return, he beat me with three switches at one time, causing me to have bruises and welts all over my body. When my mother came home, I showed her the marks. When she confronted my uncle, he told her she should've been home to watch her own children. Then they started arguing. My mother, no stranger to being on the receiving end of a physical confrontation, went in a different direction and took out a warrant against him. I remember going to the police station, but I don't remember the outcome; I was just too young to understand.

One thing I did understand then, and I know for certain now: no child should be abused or tortured. The Bible says children are a gift from the Lord; they are a reward from him. (Psalm 127:3 NLT)

Looking back, my mom was kind of 'slick,' saying what she thought people wanted to hear in order to get her way. I don't know for certain, but I imagine alcohol and drugs played a factor. My mother got into another abusive relationship . . . and another . . . and another. Some of these abusive relationships sent her to the hospital from beating after beating.

As I got older, I figured out these beatings were often because of her boyfriends' jealousies. One of her relationships left her in the hospital, bloody and unrecognizable. Her whole face was covered in blood and debris. Her boyfriend beat her up along a wooded path, stomping her, dragging her, punching and kicking her in her ribs so hard they fractured. Repeatedly, he slammed her down onto the ground and left her for dead. Time after time, as a child, that did something to me. To see my mother in need of help and not being able to help her. But she would always go back to her abuser.

I started seeing less and less of my mother to the point I was being solely raised by my grandparents. My grandmother was only nice when she was sober (which wasn't often), and my grandfather was always mean. The one thing I can never remember growing up with is love: hugs and kisses were nonexistent, laughing had to be hidden, and happiness was never felt.

My childhood was dark, cold, and . . . spooky. I can't really explain the last part, other than that's the feeling I often felt. Being hungry and living in fear was, for me, spooky. Eerie. Otherworldly.

I remember going to school just to eat. The kids would tease me about the way I smelled and my hair being knotty and matted. I used to fight or get in trouble often, lashing out against their teasing. As punishment for *my* behavior, I would be sent to the time-out corner where I soon discovered all the kids' lunch boxes were nearby on a shelf. So, while I was in time-out, I would eat their lunches. At least until I got caught.

CHAPTER 4

Woodstock Elementary: Five Years Old

I attended Woodstock Elementary in Virginia Beach. The school was collecting nonperishable canned goods for needy families for Thanksgiving. One year, I took a rusty can out of one of our cabinets to donate to the United Way and, to my surprise, that same can came right back to our house as a donation. That's when I first learned we were one of the poor families the school was collecting for. We also benefited from the United Way at Christmastime. When we did eat, I remember standing up at the kitchen table (because we didn't have kitchen chairs) or sitting on the floor.

The struggle was real. We couldn't even afford second-hand clothes. I remember going behind the local thrift store looking for clothes to wear from the people who dropped bags off after hours. Food was scarce, so I had to be creative: I took to eating out of the kitchen trashcan in our house (usually the leftover food my granddaddy threw away when he was full); "dumpster diving" (eating discarded expired food from the dumpsters behind Be-Lo's grocery store and the neighborhood Tastykake warehouse); sucking the 'honey' from honey suckle trees; eating crab apples from trees and snake berries from the grass; and drinking sugar water.

One of the reasons I was sure I was hated was the way my grandmother and mother both combed my hair. They would harshly comb through my hair starting from the root and pulling through all the tangles and knots, pulling clumps of my hair out. If I cried or put my hand up in pain, they would slap my hand with the comb.

One Easter, my mother found a pretty dress for me. I was so excited the day before to wear a dress on Easter with my hair in bows like all the other little girls on Easter Sunday. She put the dress in a dresser downstairs by the front door.

Later that same day, my mother left the house with no shoes on, saying she would be right back, but she drove off in a car with a man. When it was time for me to go to bed, my mother still wasn't home. During the night, I would wake to see if she was back home, but she wasn't. All through the night, I would go back to sleep and wake to look for her until it was daylight. I snuck downstairs to check the dresser to make sure the dress was still there. It was . . . just as beautiful as the first time I had seen it. It had pink lace with a bow, and it was, honestly, the most beautiful dress I had ever seen. My mother never came home, and I never got the chance to wear that dress on Easter Sunday because I didn't know how to put the dress on by myself, and dressing me up wasn't a priority.

Hunger. Fear. Loneliness. Disappointment. Hatred. Worthlessness. Helplessness. This had been my life as a little girl.

CHAPTER 5

My Father's Visit

After a time, I rarely saw my mother growing up. When I did, I never really saw her with women as friends; it was always men. It could be a room full of men, and she would be the only woman. But most often, she was gone. My granddaddy was usually gone, too. But my grandmother was almost always at home, most often drunk, and sitting in her favorite chair.

My father had been drafted into the Army to fight in the Vietnam War before I was born, so I had never met him. No one on my father's side of the family came to visit me until my father came home from the war. When he came back, he soon found out about me, along with everything else that had been going on.

The first time I remember my father coming to visit me, he brought me new clothes and a bag of Munchos potato chips. Oh, how I loved those pretty clothes and those chips. They were my favorite. He lifted me up high into the sky, and twirled me around, and gave me hugs and kisses. He sat and played with me and my siblings. My father noticed my mother wasn't there. The house was cold, smelly, and dirty. So was I.

During my dad's visit, he went to a family member across the street to see what was really going on in that house where I lived. Time went by, and before I knew it, I was getting visitations from social services at school. The first day I spoke to a social worker, I was leaving school to catch the bus home, and my dad and Sylvia, (his wife at the time), were at the ramp exit door. I recognized him from a distance and ran into his arms. He picked me up in the air, hugged and kissed me, and so did his wife. The next visit from social services was at my house. The case worker knocked on the door and talked to my grandparents. My grandmother was drunk, and my mother was off with one of her boyfriends.

The case worker took me outside and put me into her car, which was parked in front of the house. She asked me questions about my living conditions. Mostly 'yes' and 'no' answers, but I do remember her asking me if I got beatings, and I said, "Yes, with belts and switches." That's when I found out my dad was fighting to get custody of me.

When the case worker left, my grandparents and uncle asked me, "What did she say? What kind of questions did she ask you?"

I was scared to tell them some of the questions she asked me because I couldn't comprehend the relevance or repercussions at that age, and I didn't understand all that the case worker was saying. My granddaddy told me to go pick a switch off the tree, and he beat me with it for not telling them everything.

Some time went by, and my dad hired a lawyer to win custody of me. My dad was in his twenties, and this was in the 1970s. Before the court date, my mom asked me who I wanted to live with, and I said her. By this time, I had five other siblings, and being the oldest, I felt responsible for them. I couldn't leave them! I loved them. *Who would take care of them? Who would protect them?* These were my thoughts, even as a young child.

> "... for I will contend with those who contend with you, and
> I will save your children." (Isaiah 49:25 ESV)

Father, thank you for your protection and safety. Thank you for dispatching your angels on my behalf, for defending, preserving, rescuing, and delivering me through evil.

In Jesus' name, Amen!

CHAPTER 6

The Day My Mother Lost Custody

Princess Anne Municipal Court House, Virginia Beach, Virginia

The day of the custody hearing, I walked into the courtroom with my granddaddy and my mother looking the best I have ever looked. My hair had been combed with love. My clothes were pretty. I had on a green shirt, green pants, white socks, and black patent leather shoes. As I sat between my granddaddy and my mom, they asked me again who I was going to choose to live with.

I said, "You, Mom!"

Minutes later, my dad waved to me from a distance and opened his arms for me to come to him, so I sat between my dad, my dad's wife, and my dad's sister, Aunt Brenda. This was the most attention I had ever had in my life. My dad also asked me who I was going to pick.

I said, "You, Dad!" (As a young child living in those conditions, I learned really quickly how to problem solve and protect myself.)

As the court case went on, I didn't understand all the things the lawyer and the social worker were saying to the judge. The next thing I knew, I was in the judge's chambers. The judge was really nice. He asked me one question that changed my whole life.

"Who do you want to live with?" he asked.

This was the first time I ever mentioned this to anyone, not even my dad or mom. My heart said my mother, but my head said my father. I told the judge I wanted to live with my father.

My father won the custody battle, and as the elevator door opened and I was getting off, I saw my mother crying, so I started to cry, too. I thought maybe I had made a mistake by choosing my dad.

I will never forget the last words out of my mother's mouth to me. "I am going to win you back!" she said.

At that moment, I felt relief from the shame and guilt I previously felt. I left the courthouse with my father, his wife, and Aunt Brenda with the knowledge that one day, my mother was going to win me back! I felt like a treasured prize!

Leaving the courthouse, I don't remember the actual ride to my new home, but I do remember pulling up to my new house in Crestwood. I walked in to see a kitchen with a table and chairs, a bathroom with running water and a tub, TVs in the rooms, working lights with heat, and my very own bedroom and closet. The first thing my dad told me to do was to take off my clothes and throw them in the trash. He had bought me a closet full of new clothes and pajamas that I'd never had. Later that day, he took me to the store because he forgot I didn't have a bathrobe to cover up with. This was the first time I ever had a toothbrush, toothpaste, and a house that functioned. I did not have to go outside to use the bathroom or to use newspaper to wipe my butt. It was actually the first of everything.

Time went on, and I met the rest of my family on my dad's side. My grandmother, Nana, was my father's mother, who lived in New Rochelle, New York, and she came to visit on special occasions. I also met my cousins. I liked my new school, B. M. Williams Elementary, and I loved my new teacher, Mrs. Roach. Life was great in my eyes, but I still missed my mom. My dad and stepmom would teach me how to pray every night before bed. We would bow on the floor by the bed and pray, thanking God and praying for others. My prayer would always include, "God bless my mother!"

I was doing great. My dad and stepmom kept me busy. I was into modeling, dancing, and for the first time, I was even doing great in school.

CHAPTER 7

Love at First Sight and Aunt Brenda

Receiving love from my new family was way different from where I came from. I have a lot of favorite moments, but I will never forget the Williams family, my dad's first wife's parents. They were so nice to me as a child. How they treated me, I had never felt that type of love before. They loved me: Granddaddy, Mama, Mama Earl, and Sylvia (when she didn't pinch me because I couldn't pronounce a word). Mama Earl would give me baths in the tub, rub my back, and lotion my body down. She was great! Mama used to always tell me how pretty I was, how beautiful I was, that my skin was so soft, and how I had pretty hands. I would always sit with her in church because Mama Sylvia (as I began calling my dad's first wife) sang in the choir. Granddaddy just spoiled me. I couldn't do anything wrong in his eyes. I truly felt loved and protected by them. They never beat me.

As time went by, I was now ten years old, and my father and my stepmom weren't getting along. I could hear them fighting in the den as I lay in bed, waiting to fall asleep. They separated for whatever reason, heading for divorce.

My dad and I moved in with Aunt Brenda, who lived down the street from us in Crestwood. Aunt Brenda always had open arms for everyone. My dad and I lived there for a good while. It was there he bought me my first bike and taught me how to ride it.

I loved living with Aunt Brenda because she had two kids, my two older cousins, Charleen and Shawn. Shawn was my favorite cousin. We played, fought, and hung out with friends, but we loved each other. My Aunt Brenda called us "the twins." My cousin, Charleen, taught me how to be settled and act like a young lady, even though I didn't want to. I admired Charleen's relationship with Aunt Brenda. I always wanted to lie in bed with my mother and pillow talk, hug, kiss, and have her tickle me, like they did. I wanted my mother to do my hair, dress me up, lotion me down, and teach me how to be a young lady, like they did. Just loving me! I hungered for that attention from my mother, but it never happened in my childhood or adulthood. Still, life was so great with my new family.

One day, I told my cousin Charleen I missed my mom. I don't know how she knew where my mom was. I think my cousin had a general idea of where my mother was. So, we walked a little over a mile into a nearby neighborhood named Old Crestwood. We got to the street where my cousin thought my mom was living. Unfortunately, she didn't know the address. People stood on the corner talking, and we asked them if they knew my mother. We gave them her name, and they pointed in the direction they thought she lived. My cousin and I knocked on door after door, finally finding my mother.

She yelled from the inside, "Come in!" We walked inside and found her barefoot and drunk, unable to even stand up. She was surprised to see me, but didn't get up off the couch. She didn't even give me a hug. Our encounter was very brief. It was the first time I had seen her since the court custody case, but I remembered her saying she would fight to win me back. I held on to that as Charleen and I walked back home.

We stayed with Aunt Brenda for a while, but then my dad found us another home in another neighborhood called College Park in Virginia

Beach. Our townhouse was in a new development, and it was huge. Most houses were not that big. In College Park, I had a bigger room and bigger closet. We had a community pool that I loved. I did have to go to another school, but I met new friends in the new neighborhood.

Things were going great. At the time, it was just me and my father until he reconciled with Mama Sylvia, and she moved back in with us. Shortly after, they separated again and, eventually, got a divorce.

I really missed my mom and my siblings, not being able to see them anymore. After leaving the courthouse, my mother did not make any attempts to visit me, so my father would take me to visit her at my grandparents' house, where she would inevitably return. That's when I learned we didn't live far away from my grandparents. It was really walking distance, but I had to cross a busy highway. I was willing to take the risk.

CHAPTER 8

The Failed Reconnection

I started to visit my mother without my dad knowing; he didn't find out about my visits until later. I was in the fourth grade, attending College Park Elementary in Virginia Beach, and I walked across that busy highway to visit her before going to school. I would go to the house and comb my sister's hair, pick out my siblings' clothes for the week, then leave and go to school.

One visit traumatized me. One of my mother's boyfriends beat her up badly, and she was hospitalized for a while. It was a secret that I couldn't tell anyone because I was sneaking my visits to the house. It bothered me so bad that I couldn't focus on my schoolwork. I did tell my teacher, but she didn't understand all that I had been through. Shortly after, I ran away to find my mother to make sure she was okay. She wasn't at home, so I went knocking door to door looking for her. The first time I saw her since she had been hospitalized, she had no teeth because her boyfriend had knocked them out, and she had a cast on her arm because he had broken it. From that moment on, I wanted to protect her even more than I had before.

As I look back now, God was protecting *me* because *I* was really in danger's way.

CHAPTER 9

"Runaway"

I would constantly run away to be with my mom and my siblings. I started running away from home at the age of ten. My grades dropped; my attitude changed. I was angry, and I wanted people to feel the way I did, so I started bullying and fighting. After running away several times, I was put in a secure group home, out in the country area of Virginia Beach. I stayed there for a while until I got into a fight, and then I was sent to Tidewater Detention Center.

At the detention center, I was treated just like a prisoner. I had to strip off all my clothes from head to toe. They searched my head, hair, and ears, and then I had to bend over and cough to make sure I did not have any contraband hidden in my body. After stripping, they would 'wand' my body. I finished all my intake papers, and then I was taken to another room to shower. I had to wear their white jumpsuits, and I had to remove my shoestrings from my shoes so that I wouldn't choke myself or attempt suicide.

As the guard opened my cell door, I only had a tiny bed, a toilet, and a blurry window from which I could only see a glimpse of daylight. My cell was cold, and I was lonely. When it was time to eat, the guards would come to get me. There was absolutely no talking in the cafeteria; the punishment would be to get sent back to the cell. I talked and was sent back to my cell. Even though the food was very nasty, I was hungry, and memories of hunger from my early childhood tormented me. I learned my lesson. The next time it was mealtime, I was quiet.

CHAPTER 10

My Life of Group Homes and Detention Centers

I went to court, handcuffed and shackled with the rest of the inmates. We were put into a holding cell like prisoners until the judge was ready to hear our cases. It felt like forever that day, but I was released to go home with my father. I was so behind in my school lessons in every class. The kids in school would 'joke' me, so I began to act out in class. I started disrespecting my teachers and peers. My grades were horrible. My sixth-grade report card: five Fs and one D. I remember my father telling me I didn't have to go to school to fail!

I was so far behind in school, I didn't see a way to catch up, so I started getting into all kinds of trouble. Picking fights, stealing, selling drugs, skipping school, smoking cigarettes, bullying, fighting, and lying to cover up all of my wrongdoings. That went on from the age of ten until I was about sixteen years old. I was in and out of juvenile detention centers and secured centers where I had no freedom and was watched like a prisoner, to less secure detention centers where I did have a little freedom. But my mother did come to visit me when I was in the group home and detention centers.

I ended up going to another group home. My favorite group home was the Crisis Center on 21st Street in Virginia Beach. Most of us were in there for running away, doing drugs, or just having bad relationships with our guardians. The centers were like a home away from home with their own set of rules and curfews. We went to the regular city school and were held accountable for our actions. We went out together on outings, we went shopping, and we went to movies. I stayed there for a while, and then I was released again to go back home to my father.

Even though I didn't come with any instructions, my father did the best he could with raising me. No one in my family tried to understand why I was acting out. I had come from a home with an outhouse, no running water, no bathroom, no shower, no toilet, and sharing a bedroom with five other siblings. I was dirty, smelled foul, and felt ugly. I then went to a new home with my own clean room and everything I could dream of, but no one understood why that wasn't enough. I wanted my mother and my siblings. They were together, and I was apart from them.

Back at my father's house, I started running away again. My father started punishing me by beating me with belts, switches, and extension cords. I remember the day my dad ripped a cord from the iron and started whaling on me. *Abuse is wrong!* I thought then, and I know for sure now.

But I still ran away, in search of love from my mother.

I got all kinds of butt-beatings when it came to my education: for not understanding my homework, and for not knowing how to read or pronounce words correctly. I also got beatings and was put on punishment for not getting my math problems right. Lying, stealing, fighting, and running away led to forging my dad's name on failed test papers and wearing my stepmom's clothes and makeup to school. It just didn't matter what I did, so I did whatever I wanted to do. I felt I had no one on my side. I had a stepbrother, Lamar, but we weren't close. I never had anyone to sit me down and invest in me. Name it, I was punished for it. I didn't feel loved, valued, or wanted. Just as I felt abandoned and abused living with my mother, I felt the same with my father. I learned as a little girl that love is abuse.

CHAPTER II

Lonely

I hated my life. I thought many times of committing suicide. *I hated me!* I felt like I couldn't do anything right. It was me against the world. I really couldn't hurt myself, so the closest I came was drinking shampoo, like that was going to end my life, and snorting fingernail polish. It all just made me sick.

I didn't have anyone I could talk to who would understand me. The only thing that made me happy was running track. I was in the seventh grade at Brandon Middle School in Virginia Beach, and I was the best runner. But that was short-lived because I got into trouble in school, so my father took that sport away from me and never allowed me to try out again.

After not being able to run as part of a team, I was angry, and I didn't care about anything or anyone. I was supposed to be the next Wilma Rudolph track star. I do believe that if I had been given another chance of trying out for track, my story would have been very different. Running track was all I cared about, and I was the fastest, and at the time it gave me the positive attention I craved. When that was taken away from me, everything from that point in life went downhill.

Soon after, I ran away from home again. Lonely, down and out, I stayed in the woods, not sure where I was going because my grandfather told me not to come back. That night, I walked from College Park, where I lived, to Level Green, a nearby neighborhood about five miles away, where my middle school bus driver's house. It was late at night, and the school bus was close by, so I trespassed, pried open the school bus door, and stayed on the bus and slept. That night, I was freezing, trembling to my bones. I had run away and didn't bring a coat. It had been a nice, pleasant temperature during the day, but at night, the temperature dropped drastically. I was freezing and unsure of my next move.

I happened to look out the window, and I saw a neighbor looking at the bus. She told my bus driver, who came on the bus and got me off. I told her I had run away from home and was freezing, so she allowed me inside her home and gave me a blanket and some hot cocoa. Afterward, she called the police, and the police notified my dad.

The police took me to Virginia Beach Intake, where I had to talk to my probation officer, Mr. Tateman. Because it was the weekend, I had to wait until Monday to see the judge. So, I was taken to a secure group home out in the country of Virginia Beach. I was so familiar with all the group homes that I felt like I was at home. During this time, I would have rather been at the group homes than at my own home because I felt safe. I went to court, and the judge was concerned about my frequency of running away from home, so he took me back to his chambers. I told the judge that I missed my mother and siblings and that my dad beat me. I was sent to Tidewater Regional Group Home off of Laskin Road in Virginia Beach.

Again, my home away from home. I started to love the group homes because they didn't abuse me. I felt heard and loved. Even if the counselors were pretending, they did a wonderful job improving my self-worth.

My father had his hands full with me. I was going to Lynnhaven Middle School until I got suspended for fighting a girl in my class. I'm not sure why we were fighting, probably just something for me to do. The next day, the girl I fought brought her older sister to the school to fight me, but I beat up her sister, not knowing then that it *wasn't* her sister . . . it was actually her mother. I went to court for assault, but the judge dropped the charges because her mother was trespassing when she came to confront me on school grounds.

CHAPTER 12

Haunted House

I was sent back home to my father; soon, very soon, I got into trouble again at school. My father didn't know what to do with me. He only knew what worked for him, so there I was again getting beaten with a belt. To try to 'scare me straight,' my dad put a knife to my neck. I froze and didn't move. He put the knife down and walked out of my room, leaving me in suspense. I didn't know what to do or to expect next. Within minutes, my dad was snoring, so I knew he was asleep. Only then did I feel safe and at ease, like I could finally breathe.

I *really* hated myself and my life. I didn't have a childhood. All of what I went through from a little girl to almost turning fifteen was supposed to be love. If love was a punching bag, then I didn't want it. I had a mother who abused, abandoned, and rejected me, and a father who said he loved me but physically abused me for not knowing what wasn't taught to me. Math, reading, history, all my schoolwork, or out of his own anger and frustration. I was bringing home failing report cards for a reason.

Did I have a learning disability? Why was I running away from home? My dad did *not* take the time out to listen to me or to understand me, and why I was failing my grades or running away. My dad's second wife (my new stepmom) didn't help me either; she just stayed out of it.

I needed my mother to care about me, or someone to help me. To listen to me, to hold my hand, to give me hope. To realize I was going through a lot. Someone to guide me and direct me, in a loving way, without judgment, threats, punishments, or abuse.

The 'straw that broke the camel's back' was the day I got into a fight at school and was suspended. My dad was trying to beat me with a belt, and I was blocking the hits with my hands. He snapped. He punched me and knocked my two top front teeth backwards. Blood started gushing everywhere. My dad was so apologetic. He called the dentist immediately. I went to the dentist, and the dentist pulled my teeth forward to my gums that had been knocked back. *Boy, was it painful!* I had to wear braces for a while to correct my teeth. My dad apologized to me and said he would never hit me again, and he didn't. He even took me out to buy new clothes. A couple of days later, for no reason I could articulate, I packed my suitcase and ran away for the last time, looking for my mother.

I searched for my mother again until a friend of hers told me that she was in the hospital because another one of her boyfriends had beaten her up. I went to a friend's house, but I stayed in the woods by a ditch until daylight. After finding my mom and spending time with her, the police came and picked me up because my father reported me as a runaway, and he knew where I would be.

The officers took me to Virginia Beach Intake again, where they now knew me by name. I was admitted into Tidewater Detention Home (TDH), so I couldn't run away before my court date. After court, I was admitted to Tidewater Regional Group Home again.

"Train up a child in the way he should go, and when he
is old, he will not depart from it." (Proverbs 22:6 KJV)

"These commandments that I have given you today are to be on your hearts. Impress them on your children. Talk about them when you sit at home and when you walk along the road, when you lie down and when you get up." (Deuteronomy 6:6-7 NIV)

They say if it doesn't kill you, it will make you stronger. I am a parent now, and I see that, as parents, we all make mistakes. Without making excuses for my own parents, I understand their actions better now.

Diligently spend time with your child educating them on God's word and living out the truth before them. When we don't use the Holy Bible for instructions, that's when we rely on past experiences and what was done to us. That's when children can become mistreated, neglected, abandoned, and abused by those God has entrusted to their care. And despite my experiences, not every group home has the same kind of love, care and understanding that built up my self-esteem. Hopefully, this can help the next person, like it helped me.

CHAPTER 13

Job Corps

As my father was visiting me at a group home, he told me about a flyer he saw that said 'Job Corps.' It was a school for kids like me, ages sixteen through twenty-one. My father took down the information from the flyer, called the intake officer, and set everything up so that I could learn a trade, get my GED, and learn some discipline. The only problem was that I had to wait until I turned sixteen years old.

Well, everything worked out. Shortly after turning sixteen, I went into Job Corps. They paid for my Greyhound bus ticket, and I was sent on my way to Charleston, West Virginia. I was the youngest there; there weren't many sixteen-year-olds. Almost everyone was eighteen or older. *I loved it!* I was independent, though I shared a room with my roommates. It was like being at college away from home.

I didn't get into too much trouble in Job Corps, but I did have a scare with a man on the outside. Men used to hang around the outside of the campus searching to devour and manipulate innocent girls. I met one man who was really nice to me, and he let me drive his car without having my license. Being young and naïve, he took me to his house, he said, "just to grab something." He told me to come in and sit on the bed to cool off, but really only to try to have sex with me. Somehow, I fought my way out of his house and walked back to the Job Corps Center. I didn't report him because I believed I was in the wrong for going with him, but I did tell my roommates. The man still came by the campus, but I ignored him and looked the other way whenever I saw him.

While in Job Corps, I received my first job at sixteen years old, working at Long John Silver's, making $3.25/hour. My second job in West Virginia was working as an in-home companion for an older couple.

I was in Job Corps for two years before I was dishonorably discharged in 1988. I failed my GED test and all my academic classes, along with too many unexcused absences from class. But I did receive my driver's license through driver education there. Yeah . . . me in the winter, driving up and down the snowy hills and mountains of West Virginia had been my biggest accomplishment.

Although I was eighteen and done with Job Corps, I still felt like a failure. My last grade before going to Job Corps was a failing grade, and I had never been to high school. The year that all my friends were going to high school, I was discharged for missing too many days and my failing grades. I had dropped out of public school, failed Job Corps for my trade (which was offset printing), and I had failed to get my GED. I didn't graduate with my high school class in Virginia, and I didn't graduate with my Job Corps classmates. I remember crying all the way to the bus station when the guard was taking me to be dropped off. I got my luggage from the van, went inside to get my ticket, and as I was waiting for them to call my bus, I just cried. I cried and slept the whole way home.

When I got back to Norfolk, Virginia, I was picked up by my father, and I learned he had purchased a home in Georgetown in Chesapeake, Virginia, not too far from where we originally lived. It was a nice house, but I didn't feel at home or welcome.

My stepbrother, Lamar, had gone into the military, and when he came back on leave, his 'welcome home' was always his favorite meal. My 'welcome home' was "don't touch this" and "don't touch that." My dad was so strict, and I didn't feel like I fit in; I actually felt like I was in prison. I don't remember having any favorite days or favorite birthdays until I was in my 40s, and I thank my neighbor, Mrs. Eason, for that gift.

CHAPTER 14

Becoming an Adult

One day out of the blue, at the age of eighteen, I woke up hopeless in my new room, feeling like I was inside a prison cell. I didn't see a future for myself, so I packed my clothes, called a cab, and left my father's house with no desire or intention to return. The cab took me to where my siblings were. Since I was eighteen and legally an adult, I knew the police wouldn't come to pick me up for running away and take me back home. My childhood had been a waste.

My siblings were staying with my grandparents, while my mother was living with her boyfriend, a different man, next door. My siblings were happy to see me, and I was happy to see them. My mother came to see me. She hadn't seen me in two years, not since she visited me in the group home, and I don't recall her even giving me so much as a hug, but I do remember her saying, "How many times are you going to run away?"

I learned a lot that time around about my mother. As I got older, she would speak negatively about me to other friends and family members. She wouldn't take up for me, she wouldn't support me. She hated me, it seemed. When I asked her why she didn't fight for me like she promised me, she repeatedly said that she wished she hadn't had me. I knew she was drunk when she made those awful comments to me, but as her daughter, it would always break my heart. At that point, I didn't know what love was, other than pain. I thought to myself, what, actually, is love?

Love is abusive!

Love is lonely!

Love is sadness!

Love is hungry!

Love stinks!

Love is living in fear!

Love is abandonment!

I didn't realize it then, growing up, but I was living a true example of generational curses. Deep down, my biological parents were really sweet people, but 'life' lived from past generations led to their generational issues. Mental healthcare in the '40s, '50s, '60s, '70s, and '80s was near nonexistent. Family counseling wasn't like it is today for parents and children.

On a hot summer day, while sitting on the front porch of my grandparents' house, my father came to visit to see how I was doing. He didn't have many words to say to me, but I do remember him saying that I had to do more with my life . . . more than just existing.

After my father left, my brothers were playing, and one of them tossed their black Converse sneaker in the air, and it wrapped around the wire on the telephone pole in front of our house. Moments later, God showed me a vision of children running in and out of that shoe and in and out of the shoelaces. They were sliding down the tongue of the shoe: cheerful, happy, laughing. The vision was in color like 'the old lady who lived in the shoe' nursery rhyme. I was eighteen years old when God gave me that vision, but I didn't pay much attention to it then. I just thought it was my imagination playing with me.

As months went on, things started to turn sour with me being at my grandparents' house. They talked about me, saying they didn't want me there anymore. I wasn't welcome. I had to ask for everything, even a glass of water to drink. My mother, who I thought would take up for me, only talked about me, too. That *really* hurt because my whole childhood, my whole *life*, had been spent chasing my mother's love.

I was working at a local Long John Silver's restaurant when I found out my father had been paying my grandfather for letting me stay there in the past, but he had stopped paying because I had turned eighteen years old, and it was my decision, my choice, to be there. Now I knew why everyone was turning their backs on me. I had to move on.

CHAPTER 15

Moving On

I decided to move in with my mother's baby brother, my gay uncle, and his lesbian girlfriend in Huntersville, a neighborhood in Norfolk, Virginia. I rented a room from them for $35.00/week. I transferred my job to a Long John Silver's that was closer to the bus route in Norfolk to make sure I could get back and forth to work. I stayed there for a while, but I soon grew tired of all of the fighting, the drag queen shows, and the round-the-clock drinking. Besides all that, my room was roach-infested. Still, I didn't want to go back to my father's house with all his strict rules and me feeling like I was back in prison again. Freedom and love were what I was after.

Most girls are 'Daddy's girls.' I was a Daddy's girl until my father got his first divorce. Before that, my father was nice to me. We would wrestle, and he would teach me how to fight, and he would tickle me and carry me on his back. We would laugh! He would throw me in the air, twirl me around, give me big ole hugs and kisses! And then I lived in fear of him.

I heard family members talk about his PTSD, Post-Traumatic Stress Disorder, and I knew he had been drafted into the Vietnam War. I believe that was one reason why my life was hell. I contemplated suicide many times, but I wasn't strong enough to really hurt myself.

CHAPTER 16

My First Boyfriend

One day, I decided to go back to visit my siblings; that is where I met my first boyfriend, Charles. He was hired as a subcontractor to work on the house we grew up in, running electricity and plumbing throughout. He was tall and light-skinned, like my mother, and he thought I was beautiful. We exchanged numbers and became very good friends. He was twenty-seven years old, and I was nineteen. He told me he had just gotten out of a relationship and wasn't looking to get into anything serious. At the time, I didn't know he was on drugs. I just knew he gave me the attention I always wanted.

As time went by, things weren't working out with my uncle, with all the fighting and the drinking and the mice. One day, I asked my boyfriend if I could stay with him, just for two weeks. Although he said he wasn't looking for a relationship, he allowed me to stay. That two-week stay ended up being eight years in total.

My boyfriend and I later moved to Academy Park in Portsmouth, Virginia; it wasn't the best neighborhood, but it was better than the original place. I worked two jobs, and my father cosigned for me to buy a reliable car.

One day, I felt a flutter and asked my mother why something was moving in my stomach; she said it was probably a "rolling tumor." A few weeks later, the movement increased more and more. When I got off work, I went to the hospital and told the nurse that something was moving in my stomach. They ran some tests, came back to me, and said, "Ms. Reid, you are seven-and-a-half months pregnant!"

I was in shock! I had no idea I was pregnant, or that becoming pregnant was even possible, because I had been told by doctors that I couldn't have children. When I found out about the pregnancy, my boyfriend was in jail for driving on a suspended license. When he was able to call home, I told him that I was seven-and-a-half months pregnant. He remembered that night clearly. Six weeks later, at the age of twenty-two, I had my son, Brian. It was October 1991, and all I had at the time for my son was a pair of booties. When I left the hospital, I went to my father's house, and he bought everything we needed. I only stayed with my father a couple of days, and then I went home.

Because I was so far into my pregnancy when I found out, I hadn't saved up any money and needed to go back to work soon to be able to take care of myself and my child. I was ready to go back to work, but I had to wait until I got a doctor's release. Time went on, and my boyfriend and I moved to a better home to raise our son. Things were going really well with us for a while, until my boyfriend started drinking heavily and doing drugs. He was in and out of jail, losing his job, and stealing. But I stayed.

When my son was about four years old, we moved to College Park in Virginia Beach, into the same townhouse where I grew up with my father. At that time, my boyfriend's oldest two children from his previous marriage came to live with us. Their mother was tired and wanted him to take some responsibility, and at the time, things were going pretty well between us. I was working around the clock, and even though he was working also, his paycheck wasn't reflecting the number of hours he was supposedly working. We started getting behind in our rent. I would come home, and my stereo and speakers would be gone. Microwave, tools, lawn mowers, anything of value? Gone. My boyfriend had pawned them and was getting more and more hooked on drugs. My life was going downhill fast. Eventually, his kids went back home to their mother, and he ended up moving to Florida for a job.

My son and I moved to Georgetown. This time it was just me and my son, Brian, separating ourselves from the drugs, lying, and mistrust. By the time Brian was five years old, we had moved four times.

At this time in our lives, I was working at Applebee's as a line cook. I was interested in management, and the store manager, Smitty, took an interest in me. He guided me and showed me all that I needed to learn to fulfill the role. I started off as a line cook. I would come in and open up the kitchen. Slowly, he began to give me more and more responsibilities, as well as constructive criticism to make me better. Smitty basically took me under his wing.

I ended up being transferred to another Applebee's as a Manager in Training, and finally, in 1996, I was promoted to manager. If it wasn't for Smitty seeing something in me, I don't know where I would be today with no education.

The fact that I had dropped out of middle school, failed Job Corps, and failed my GED test weighed heavily on me. The day I was promoted to manager was the happiest day ever. I was so excited! That day was a total surprise to me. I went to work to see the schedule that was posted weekly. I looked for my name, and it wasn't there. I went to my store manager and asked why my name wasn't on the cook's schedule. That's when he told me I had been promoted. I screamed, and then I cried. I was so proud of myself; I did something right. Barely any education, and now I was the kitchen manager for Applebee's Bar and Grill. During the '90s, Applebee's was the real deal. Being in management taught me how to run a business. It taught me teamwork, accountability, and responsibility.

This was God's perfect plan!

"And we know that all things work together for good to those who love God, to those who are the called according to his purpose." (Romans 8:28 NKJV)

All things, including my failures, my mistakes, and even the attacks of the devil, were all a part of God's perfect plan for my life.

I loved my job and always wanted to know more about the business. I worked as a manager for Applebee's for over ten years, and I enjoyed the ride and the experience. I called it "my experience," or should I say, my on-the-job training. During those years, I was transferred to other locations to share my experiences. I traveled and filled in at other locations when other managers were on vacation or were out sick. I finally had skills, knowledge, and responsibilities worthy of respect.

Although this was one of the happiest seasons of my life, it was also one of the saddest. My mother passed away, and my boyfriend and I were officially over due to his drug addiction. Even though I was promoted and making more money, I still struggled as a single mother. I was already behind on my bills, so pitching in to bury my mother was a financial hardship.

The irony was, she had money to bury herself; there was a policy at the bank in both our names awarded from Social Security. But at some point, she took my name off the policy and added her boyfriend's name. After her death, he ran off, taking the money from the policy and whatever little money she had. My siblings and I were left to split the bill to properly bury her. Applebee's, more than just my place of employment, raised money for my family, and they even provided food for my family as we gathered before the funeral to have visitors.

During this time, I really struggled. I knew, but I didn't fully understand the magnitude of the loss I had suffered. I was going through depression, and I was grieving. Often, I found myself reflecting back on my mother's life and the relationship we had or didn't have. Even though I was only twenty-seven years old when she died, I felt as though she had already died back when I was a toddler. Even when we had been together, it was like her body had left this earth because her presence didn't matter to me any longer. I couldn't depend on her to protect me. I hadn't felt loved, or even wanted, by her. She abandoned me repeatedly. In the midst of my grieving, bitterness had started to enter my heart.

Fortunately, and only by the grace of God, this truly was one of my turnaround moments. I received another promotion at work, and I had really worked very hard for it. Nothing was given to me, which made me appreciate my efforts even more. I worked on my days off, I came in early, and I rarely left on time, routinely working past the end of my shift. I wanted to learn more about management, leadership, and how to run a business. I wanted the position more than the position wanted me! I went after everything I needed to do. I *saw* myself as a manager before I was a manager. I *promoted* myself within myself. I've learned that for most things in life, you have to pursue your dream as you envision it, before you can actually become it, with positive and controlled thoughts that will lead to positive actions. Your thoughts, negative or positive, will control your actions, and your actions have consequences, good and bad.

I became a manager through sheer determination and a made-up mind to be a better person. I had to learn patience with myself and give myself grace because it took me longer to catch on to tasks, especially during my training as an M.I.T. (Manager in Training). Through the whole process, I discovered I was a visual learner. (Please do *not* put a book in front of me because that is *not* the way I learn, and I won't get it.) The way I learn, along with all the chaos of my home life, played a major role in why I failed in school during my childhood, which mainly consisted of reading information and repeating the information through writing without any critical thought or application. I learn by seeing and doing.

After being patient with myself and learning from my mistakes, I became consistent and persistent. I disciplined myself through sacrifices and perseverance to become an associate manager. The day that happened was my graduation to life! I finally accomplished something, and I was so happy. The last grade I completed in school was the eighth grade, and I didn't receive my GED until I was thirty-seven years old. What I can say with confidence is that I never gave up!

After all of the excitement wore off, I was still driving my old car, a 1985 Cadillac Deville. I loved that car (even though it needed a jump from time to time). One day, I had gotten off from work and was ready to go home, but the car wouldn't start because the battery was dead. I went back inside the restaurant to ask if someone could help me. I will never forget, one manager said, "Robin, you are a manager now . . . go and buy yourself a dependable car."

Well, my car was paid for, so why would I want to go and make another bill? I just needed a jump every once in a while.

The next day, I had to deposit the restaurant's money into the bank. When I left the bank to go back to work, once again, my car wouldn't start. I had to wait for a jump.

My management peers' perception was that managers were supposed to have the nicest cars in the parking lot and live in a nice house. At that time, that was true for all of the managers except for me. So, I went out looking for a nice, dependable car. I could only get what was available to my credit, and my credit wasn't all that good. The car wasn't the best, like the other managers, but it was better than what I had previously.

As time went on, I made some terrible choices because I thought managers were supposed to have it all together. I appeared to have it all together, but I was struggling trying to keep up with the perception of what I should have. I was broke.

Honestly, I was beyond broke. Before, I had three previous car repossessions, had been evicted four times, and was still dealing with the grief of my mother. Now, I was a single mother struggling hard, and I could barely keep up with my car payments. I had to let my insurance lapse, and the DMV was after me for an uninsured motorist fee because I couldn't provide them with actual documented insurance. I didn't have money for either the fee or the insurance, so DMV suspended my license. So now I was a restaurant manager driving around on a suspended license without car insurance.

Because of past due electric bills from my previous addresses, my lights were cut off, and they weren't going to be turned back on until I paid the entire past due balance, which was over $800.00. I didn't even have $80 to my name. My son and I sat in the dark with candles, with him asking me why we were sitting in the dark and why the TV wouldn't come back on. As a mother, I was so embarrassed, so I told him someone had hit the electric pole. My son looked out the window and said, "Why do the neighbors across the street have lights?" I lied and told him it was only this side of the condos that the outage affected. Then I turned my head from him and let the tears run down my face.

Shortly after, my wages were garnished for the repossession of the cars, unpaid rent, and personal property taxes. The next week, frustrated, I went to my bank to withdraw money from my account. I went to the ATM, stuck in my card, and entered my PIN. Immediately, the machine took my card, and then a message flashed across the screen saying I would need to call a certain number. Without my money or my ATM card, I left and called the number. I was told my account had been frozen because another bank had summoned me to court for an unpaid car loan. I had moved, gotten evicted, and didn't change my address, so I never received the initial summons; when I didn't appear in court, the judge ordered my account to be frozen until I made arrangements to satisfy the debt. Of course, I couldn't make arrangements because I didn't have any money.

With all that I was going through, no one knew. I didn't ask for help. I kept it all to myself. I didn't even tell my father because I had made this bed hard, now I would simply have to lie in it and work it out myself. I sowed into bad ground, and I had to reap out of bad ground.

I also didn't ask my father because my house phone was cut off, and I had to call him from a pay phone. I believe he knew my situation, but he wanted me to figure it out for myself. If he knew I was calling from a pay phone and wasn't going to offer to help pay for my phone bill, I didn't have the guts to ask for anything else.

One thing that I learned from my father growing up was to have a good work ethic and to be a woman of my word. I was so reliable that one day I overslept, and when my job couldn't get in touch with me, they began calling hospitals and jails because they knew something serious had to have happened that would cause me to miss work. Even with my strong work ethic, I still struggled, but I didn't give up. Around the year 2000, I was forced to file for bankruptcy, which released the money in my bank account and relieved me of the wage garnishments. Finally, I would be able to get myself back on track.

I didn't know God then like I do now. Then, I had no relationship with Him, and I didn't know what hope was, but I had determination and perseverance. I was determined to be a great person. I was determined to have a better life than my mother. I was determined to give my son a better life. Through all I had been through, giving up wasn't an option. I am a fighter, I knew that about myself, and I was going to get it worked out.

CHAPTER 17

Moving from Portsmouth to Las Gaviotas Back Taxes: God is Good

I was looking for a simple, basic life. No frills, no fancy car. I just wanted a life with the basic necessities; a simple life of a single mother supporting herself and her son. *Why was it so hard?*

I finally had to ask for help, so my son went to live with my father and stepmom, his grandparents, for several years until I could get myself together and adequately provide. It was one thing for me to be in the dark, but he deserved better, and I remembered the days of growing up without essential heat, electricity, or running water. I would not let my son have those same childhood memories.

My son's father was still in Florida, on drugs, and wasn't helping me or paying child support. He was very intelligent and very knowledgeable of almost all trades. I can honestly say he was simply great at most things, especially electrical and plumbing work. There is no doubt in my mind that he could have easily been a Master Electrician and owned his own electrical company. Or any trade business. But drugs truly ruined his life. Even though I didn't know God *then* the way that I know Him *now*, I am so thankful that He kept me away from that lifestyle, and I can honestly say I have never experimented with any drugs. God always provided, and this time was no exception.

Although I was taught about having a strong work ethic and being a person of my word, I wasn't taught about being financially responsible. I knew nothing about budgeting and saving. I knew nothing about running a household or paying bills, much less paying tithes. *Just save a dollar for a rainy day,* was all I had ever heard.

Finally, I had a good job, and, like everyone else, I had to file taxes. One year, I went to have my taxes done, like I always did, but this particular year, I was told I owed a couple thousand dollars. I was confused and puzzled because nothing had really changed with respect to my tax status. *So why did I owe? And why did I owe so much?* I got scared, and I didn't file my taxes for five years.

But one thing I do know: Do *not* play with the IRS! In my fifth year, I decided that whatever I owed, I would simply make arrangements to pay before the IRS garnished my wages and froze my bank account again. Begrudgingly, I went to file five years of back taxes with another tax preparer. This tax preparer put in all the numbers and informed me I was getting a refund from the first year. They kept inputting the numbers for the next year and the next and the next and the next. Not only did I get a refund for the first year, but a refund for each of the years I hadn't filed, *plus interest.*

> "With man this is impossible, but with God all things are possible." (Matthew 19:26 NIV)

Still giddy from having just received my income tax refund, I drove through the neighborhood of Las Gaviotas. As I got to the townhouse on the end, I saw a man hanging a 'For Rent' sign. I parked my car, got out, and asked the gentleman if the house was still for rent. He said 'yes' and that they had just finished remodeling and painting it. He asked me if I was interested in it, and I told him 'Yes.' He asked me about my credit, and I told him it wasn't good. He said that if I wanted it, I would have to put down a deposit, first month's rent, and last month's rent. Three whole payments before I could even move in. Instead of being overwhelmed, I thought to myself, *Wow, God is good!* I told him I had all the money, and he allowed me to go inside and view the home. The townhouse was an end unit with a big front and back yard, and it also had a deck. It was closer to my job. It had two bedrooms and one and a half bathrooms, which was big enough for me and my son. I was eager to have us both back under one roof.

I loved the townhouse! It was nice inside and outside, and it was in a great neighborhood. Because I had moved five times in six years, my brother jokingly told me that if I moved again, I was on my own. Previously, I didn't have to hire help because I already had enough help from my brothers. This time, though, I hired a reasonably affordable moving company. They did all of the work, including putting my furniture together, hooking up my washer and dryer, and putting the boxes in each room where they belonged. This was truly a blessing and a great decision for my son and me. As I did a walk-through of the old condo and settled into our new home, things started to turn around for the good.

Because of my hardships and struggles, my son's grandparents allowed him to stay with them in order to give him a solid foundation, as well as time for me to get myself together as a single mother. Around 2003, my son and I moved back together as a family.

Time went on, as usual, and my son was doing great in school, playing football, and taking up karate. He had made friends in the neighborhood and at his school. As a football player, he was popular and enjoying life as he should. He was going to football games, hanging out with friends, camping, going to sleepovers and parties, and doing lots of other things young teenagers should enjoy. We were finally happy!

Because I still worked so much, my son was often home alone after school. We had a plan: he had to call me when he got home from school, and he couldn't go outside until he did all of his homework and chores. Then he had to call me back at work when he was back in the house for the evening. My son was fifteen now, and he sounded so grown-up and was so handsome! I trusted him when he called that he would stay in the house, and lock the doors, take a shower, and get ready for the next day of school. But nope! Typical teenager. He would sneak back outside, and when I would call back home, he would say he had been asleep when actually he was having fun outside the whole time. One of his so-called friends actually broke into our house one time while he was outside playing basketball and stole his Nintendo set from his bedroom. He had me actually thinking about getting a babysitter for him when I worked nights, but who needed a babysitter at the age of fifteen?

During this season of my life, I was a kitchen manager and still working for Applebee's. Every Monday, we would get a delivery of products, and as the kitchen manager, one of my responsibilities was to unload the delivery truck. I had to take the boxes and cases, load them onto a dolly hand truck, and check off the merchandise, while the cooks would wheel and push the products inside the store to different locations and put them away. From doing this over a long period of time, I ended up hurting my back. Normally, when my back went out, I could bounce back in a day or so, but because of the severity of the injury this time, I was out of work on workman's comp at least three or four times over a period of years. The last time I injured my back was the last time I was out of work, and it was so bad that I was now unable to work.

I stayed home with my son, and even though I was in pain, there was to be no more sneaking out while I was at work. As an adult, I had always worked, and I always had a job, so this was the only time that I had so much time on my hands. Going to medical appointments and physical therapy still kept me pretty busy. I also had to report to unemployment that I was looking for a job within my restrictions. No luck with that! No company wanted to hire me and take a risk with my injury.

Something was missing from my life. I should've been happy, but I wasn't. I decided to go back to church. I felt I was carrying a dead weight that needed to fall off of my shoulders. Being in the church played a happy chapter in my life. Once that weight started falling off, I began to feel good about myself. I loved the church so much that I got baptized and joined the church. I went to the New Members class, and, in 2005, I received my New Members certificate from 'The Mount,' signed by Bishop Kim and Elder Valerie Brown at Mount Lebanon Baptist Church in Chesapeake, Virginia.

Time went on, and I was still on workman's comp and home every day with my son. I enjoyed going to watch him play football on Thursday evenings and having fun with his friends. After about six months of not working, I became pregnant with my second child. My daughter was born on October 26th at Chesapeake General Hospital. My children were sixteen years apart. I was almost thirty-seven years old, and during my thirty-seventh year, I finally got my GED.

I now had two children: a sixteen-year-old son and a newborn daughter. Her father, much like my son's father, was otherwise occupied by many things, and he was in and out of our relationship.

I knew I had to really get myself together. I had moved seven times before my son turned sixteen years old. I had just received my GED, was working in management, but still in debt, behind on my bills, and had a poor credit score. A single mother with two wonderful children. Brian, my oldest at sixteen, and my daughter, an infant. Two different children, two different fathers, and never married.

I remember thinking to myself, *I've got to do better because I can't keep living like this. What am I going to do?* I remembered the saying, "if you always do what you've always done, you will always get what you've always gotten." I knew I had to make a change because if I didn't choose to change, then I was choosing for nothing to change. Every journey starts with a single step, and every productive day begins with a clear vision.

CHAPTER 18

My Second Child

Being a new mother again was harder the second time than the first time. It took me two years to get a hold of my daughter and establish a routine. During that time, I was secretly falling into post-partum depression, and I took a lot of my anger out on my teenage son.

Brian, if I haven't told you, I apologize for my poor behavior and poor leadership toward you. I was confused, angry, and bitter that life wasn't going great for me. It seemed like I was going in reverse. I took two steps forward and six steps backward. The people in my life were a reflection of my poor choices. There's a saying, "If you make your bed hard, you have to lie in it," meaning that by my choices and actions, I had to accept the consequence of unpleasant results. I accept full responsibility, Brian, and I hope you have forgiven me for my many mistakes.

CHAPTER 19

Unforgiveness

At this time, I still hadn't forgiven my mother. I was thirty-seven years old, holding onto unforgiveness because of her abandonment of me, and for not being in my life and in the lives of my children. I have had plenty of women who have played the role of mother to me, and I am so grateful. But I needed love from *my* definition of what I needed my mother to be. Her love just didn't seem real because I felt like there were conditions on her love. I wanted that deep, unconditional love I witnessed with others: the mommy/daughter pillow talks, the sharing secrets, the mirror talks, the giggles and laughter, the hugs and kisses, the stressful mid-life crisis help . . . My Best Friend. That's what I was looking for. I have seen my mother display those traits I've always wanted with her, but it was demonstrated toward her boyfriends instead of her children.

CHAPTER 20

The Journey to Suffolk

At first, just my son and I were living in the two-bedroom, two-bathroom townhouse in the Las Gaviotas neighborhood. It was enough space for us, but then my daughter arrived, and she had to share a room with me. That was okay for the first year while she was still in a crib, but as she got older, she needed her own room. In Las Gaviotas, a three-bedroom was expensive. I hired a realtor, my first cousin, Shawn. He pulled my credit report and told me all I needed to do was pay off all of my old debt, and then I could purchase my own home. I paid off my creditors, and he helped me to get financed; we started looking for a house. It took a couple of months. The area of Chesapeake we looked in was very pricey, especially with me being a single mother. My cousin assured me that finding a three-bedroom townhouse I could afford would be tough, but completely possible.

Shawn found me a three-bedroom, two-and-a-half-bath townhouse in Suffolk, Virginia. It was further away from where I hoped to be. I didn't know anything about the Suffolk area. I just knew it was further away, a country setting, and a lot cheaper. I didn't fall in love with the townhouse at first sight. It appeared to be under some distress and needed some cosmetic work. Nothing major, just fresh paint and new flooring. It was the kind of house that would require someone to use their imagination to see the potential. But it was cheaper than any other area within Hampton Roads.

I liked the house, but I didn't like the house. The drive was out of my way to work. My son would have to transfer schools in his junior year of high school. My daughter's daycare wasn't even on the new route I'd have to take to go to work. Nothing made logical sense for me to buy this house, only the fact that it was large enough for the three of us to have our own bedrooms, and it was in my price range. After wrestling with the decision, I decided we would move to Suffolk.

My children and I closed on our new home in February 2008. I was a first-time homebuyer! My cousin helped me find a painter and a company to remove the old flooring and install new carpet. Those things made a huge difference in the house. From that point, I could see all the potential.

> "But seek first the kingdom of God and his righteousness, and all these things will be added to you." (Matthew 6:33 ESV)

CHAPTER 21

Moving to Suffolk

I knew moving to Suffolk was really out of my way, but I don't think I really understood until the day-to-day routine set in. My daughter's daycare was in the opposite direction from my job. On a good day, with no traffic, it took me two hours to drop my daughter off and get to work on time. I remember thinking, *God, please help me,* and in that moment, I remembered why I moved to Suffolk: I wanted my children to have a better environment in which to live, and I wanted a place of my own that was affordable for me.

As time went by, I was able to find another daycare closer to my home and on the way to my job. That took my morning drive time down to one hour.

At this time, I was an Associate Manager for Panera Bread. Great job and great hours. I really enjoyed working there, and I worked there for five years before getting fired.

CHAPTER 22

Getting Fired from Panera Bread

One day, just before getting off my shift, my area supervisor stopped by to speak with me.

"Do you know anything about money shortages in the drawers and the safe?" he asked.

"Yes," I told him. "It's been going on for a while. It's always to be expected that the drawers or the safe will be short on any given shift. To correct for the shortages, we just void that amount off to make the numbers add up."

I answered him honestly and explained all of my answers to his questions.

"Have you ever done it?" he asked me.

I said, "Yes."

"That's against company policy," he said.

"The store manager is well aware," I explained, "because he was the one who told us to do it."

Since the store was under investigation, the Human Resources Office was also involved. I spoke with Human Resources, and I told them the situation. The store manager was aware of all the drawers and the shortages, and he told us how to correct those shortages. He knew what we were doing and why we were doing it because it had been going on for a while. I didn't think anything of it. Forty dollars, ten dollars, three dollars. But it added up when considering all the registers were doing it, which caused us to get audited. After the discussion, I had to write a statement about what was taking place and affirm that the store manager was aware of the transactions.

I was suspended, pending investigation, for four days. My area supervisor called me and wanted to meet with me to discuss the investigation. The next day, I met with the area supervisor and the store manager together. Then my store manager told Human Resources and the investigation team that he didn't know anything about the registers or the safe being short at any time. Since I admitted to doing it, even though it had been a matter of protocol, I was fired instead of him.

CHAPTER 23

The Drive Home

After getting fired, I drove home. I was crying so hard, I had to pull over on the interstate. As I put my van in park, tears just rolled down my face like Niagara Falls. I was so hurt! I felt like I had been stabbed in the back. There was no way the store manager didn't know. There was no way the area supervisor and Human Resources believed him. Then to see the smirks on their faces as they fired me.

I thought to myself, *I gave my all to this company. Blood, sweat, and tears.* I worked on my days off with no pay because I was a salaried employee. I came in early and stayed late. I ran errands for the store on my personal time. I worked through pain, tiredness, and depression. I had dedicated my life to this job. I worked around the clock without compensation in preparation for corporate inspections because what was important to my supervisor was important to me. *This* is what I get for all of my dedication?!

First, I was in shock. Then, I was angry. I wiped my tears and drove off. At first I was hurt; now I was mad! *But what was I going to do?*

> "No weapon formed against you shall prosper, And every tongue *which* rises against you in judgment You shall condemn." (Isaiah 54:17 NKJV)

Devil, "As far as you're concerned, you were planning evil against me, but God intended it for good, planning to bring about the present result so that many people would be preserved alive." (Genesis 50:20 ISV)

CHAPTER 24

Life after Panera Bread

The next day, I woke up clueless about my next move. Restaurant management was all I knew. *Where do I go from here?* I thought. I was done with the restaurant business. *But who's going to hire me with no references?*

In that moment, God said to me, *"Remember the daycare."*

God had given me the vision and plainly spoke to me about opening up a daycare. But I didn't want to open one. I kept saying to myself, "What if a child gets hurt?"

I thought of different options: restarting my pressure washing business from years ago, going back to catering, becoming a car salesman, and on and on. As I was writing down my options, I was getting excited with hope. My daughter was four years old and about to start preschool. It hit me that my life was about to change into another chapter.

After praying, God revealed to me that He took me from my job to start a daycare. He knew I wouldn't quit on my own, so He allowed the setup. Of course, He was right. I was fiercely loyal to that job. If I hadn't been fired, I would still be there right now, today.

I wrestled with opening a daycare until one day, my cousin, Charleen, called me and said, "You should open up a daycare." I explained to her that she was my final confirmation. Immediately after we got off the phone, I called the daycare provider, Lisa, who had kept my daughter when she was two years old. Lisa is a true entrepreneur. I told her the story about me being fired and that I wanted to open up a home daycare.

Lisa was very welcoming, and she shared with me her previous experiences. She said she thought I would be perfect for this profession because of my management background in running a business. After welcoming me, she immediately started talking about how she was going to help me. She asked me some questions and told me to think of a name for my business, my hours of operation, and the age group of the children I wanted to provide care for. Lisa suggested I start out accepting all ages until I figured out what was best for me. She was a tremendous help.

I had all of my policies and procedures down, but I needed to childproof my home. But I didn't have any money. I called my dad and asked him if I could borrow

$500.00 because I was opening up a home daycare and needed toys, tables, chairs, and food. He agreed to help me.

"When do you need the money?" he asked.

"Tomorrow," I said.

My father gifted me $500.00 to open up my business. *Thank you, Dad.*

> I once was young and now am old, yet never have I seen the righteous abandoned or their children begging for bread. (Psalm 37:25 BSB)

The following day, I went to my father's house to pick up the money and went shopping for my business. Charleen voluntarily made me flyers. My son, Brian, Angel, and I walked all over the neighborhood handing out flyers. I also let all of my family and friends know, as well as everyone in my contact list, that I was opening a preschool.

(A big shout out to Brian and Angel. Thank you both for everything. We've been together since the beginning. Thank you for your commitment and for loving the children.)

Robin's Nest Home Preschool opened on September 4, 2011. This was a true new beginning. Business was slow starting out. I had more before- and after-school children, so I would feed them a hot breakfast, clean them up, and then take them to school as well as pick them up from school. To make extra money, I rolled my neighbors' trash cans out for trash pick-up on Monday nights and rolled them back in after the trash man left. I did that for two months until business picked up with more children.

The first six years, I worked under the planning council as a volunteer registered licensee for family day homes. At the time, I could have five children at one time; in 2017, the law changed, so I could only have four children at a time unless I had a state license.

I decided to become state-licensed to care for up to twelve children. I submitted my application to the City Hall Planning Commission for Zoning and Traffic Engineering. The process took about eight months, and the process for the Virginia Department of Social Services took an additional three months. After all of my hearings, I was awarded a permit to operate a home preschool for twelve children by the City of Suffolk, Zoning Administration.

With fees, renovations, and the restructuring of my home for the safety of the children, I spent several thousand dollars. The process wasn't easy, by far. As a licensed home provider, I had to go through the same tough challenges as other licensed daycare centers. It was a totally different experience caring for twelve children with one full-time Child Development Enrichment Specialist (CDES), but we did it with determination and dedication.

If it wasn't for my sister, Malinda, Robin's Nest Home Preschool wouldn't have a Human Resources professional. Malinda has been a blessing to me every step of the way. She helps me. She does all my policies and procedures paperwork, designs and upkeeps my websites, my billings, my forms, and memos. She helped create my handbooks, my curriculum, and my enrollment package.

One time, the state inspector gave me a safety violation; Malinda went to Lowe's and literally built me a gated, locked fence that goes around my air conditioning unit to keep the daycare children from sticking their fingers inside the fan. She also helped my niece, Jazz, create a blueprint of my home for my daycare business plan. (She's also typing this book!)

Yes, my sister is a jack-of-all-trades and a master of them all.

CHAPTER 25

State License

My business experience being state-licensed was both challenging and fun. I had a curriculum for each child based on their individual needs and growth. My preschool was set up like a preschool and a kindergarten class, structured by the hour, and leaving "wiggle room" for the off days when the children are overly emotional.

My age range is from two to four years old, five-years old if they didn't make it to preschool. I am state-licensed, provide first aid, MAT certified (to administer medication), CPR certified, and certified with the state USDA program. I have amazing Child Development Enrichment Specialists ("Breezy Bree" and "Sweet Tee") who help me with the children. I changed their job titles from helpers to Child Development Enrichment Specialists due to the high level of quality care they provide. We offer one-on-one tutoring on a daily basis. We teach the children sign language and table etiquette. We teach them shapes, colors, numbers, letters, patterns, and rhyming words. We provide sensory stimulation through cutting and pasting, arts and crafts, music, story time, daily group exercise, outside free time, and exploring. We even have birthday celebrations and much more! It is truly a family affair at The Robin's Nest Preschool.

I never thought I could own and operate a home business and make double the income I did while working in Corporate America. Being able to raise my daughter, now seventeen years old, a senior in high school graduating with the class of 2025, has truly been a blessing. Even though they don't believe it, the older children get, the more they need you. To assist them in figuring out their own independence and personal journey, I had to be close by during those times as a supporter and listener. That's what I needed, and that's what I am giving to my children as best I can.

I plan on working with my home preschool until my daughter graduates from high school and enters college. Then, I will open a brick-and-mortar preschool to help even more parents who are in need of *amazing* childcare services with *amazing* Child Development Enrichment Specialists.

CHAPTER 26

Breaking Every Chain

I had to end my book with Chapter 26 because that's the day my daughter, Britne, was born. I love you Brit-Brit, keep making me proud.

My son, Brian, is now thirty-three years old. I love you, Brian. He is married to his beautiful wife, Tashena (hey, girl!). I see a lot of me in you. You take very great care of my son, you go above and beyond to be a great woman, wife, and mother. You will always have my heart, and there's nothing that you can't have. Thank you for my first grandchild.

(Happy fifth birthday, Aubree, Gruma baby. I love everything about you!)

Aubree, always remember there isn't anything too expensive for you, and you can have all your godly heart desires. You have everything in you *right now* to become all you need to be. They say you act like me, but I don't see it (smile).

To everyone reading my life story, thank you for your time and your support.

To the generations now and those who come later, your pain has purpose. I wrote this book for you, so you have a map of where your bloodline comes from, so you can measure your growth as to how far we have come as a generation. It's like a family tree of the bloodline and our struggles of being mishandled, abused, rejected, broken, uneducated, and poor. But God! Please continue to break every chain. When you know who you are and where you come from, you can do better from generation to generation.

For most generations, I won't be here to see you. I'm writing this book at the age of fifty-five years old. I am the mother of Brian and Britne and I am Aubree's grandmother. Keep Robin's Nest Preschool alive. Keep moving forward in breaking every chain. Always keep God first, and you will never be last.

I love you all deeply, this generation and all the generations after me.

I would also like to leave everyone with something very valuable to my heart, to the present generation, and to later generations. I have learned this from my pastors, Harold and Brenda McPherson, at Covenant Community Church in Suffolk, Virginia, and it has tremendously blessed my life. Pass this on to your families; embed it into your hearts:

"Honor and respect God."

"Seek God first."

"Serve God first."

"Give it to God first."

If you do this first, your life will never be the same, and everything you need will be provided for. You will have favor and be abundantly blessed. Break every chain that's keeping you in bondage.

To God be the Glory!

I love you all! Make me proud!

EPILOGUE

I Love My Parents!

I hope you are encouraged by how I battled and overcame the abandonment by my mother. There was something I needed and wanted in my childhood and adulthood, but never received . . . my mother's love. She passed away when I was twenty-seven years old. I forgave her at forty years old, when I took the focus off of myself and my desires and shifted my focus to what she was going through. She was battling many demons: not being protected; verbal, mental, and physical abuse by men (including her own stepfather, in which incest was involved); indulgence in alcohol to numb her pain; and a host of other demons, just like the other women in the generations before her. She had been born into this. I forgive her for the things she did and said, and for the things she didn't do and didn't say.

My father had been drafted into the Army and was fighting for his life in the Vietnam War. As a result of the war, as a little girl, I couldn't just walk up to my father; I had to say his name from a distance to get his attention to say good night, and then give him a kiss on the cheek. I thought my dad was mean, and I hated him for his strict discipline. But he wasn't always like that. He would get upset very easily and use a loud, thundering tone of voice, like I was a soldier under his charge. My whole childhood, I felt scared. In my early adulthood, I found out that my dad suffered from post-traumatic stress disorder, or PTSD. I can now only imagine what it must have been like to have been drafted into war at the age of eighteen, soldiers lying bleeding right beside you, bodies being blown up, friends dying left and right while you're fighting for your life in a foreign country.

Now, as an adult with a different level of comprehension and empathy, I can look back and understand my father's mood swings, anger, and flashbacks with PTSD. I can understand my mother's attempt to numb her pain through men and alcohol to escape her reality of having responsibility for six kids amid such desperate poverty. A baby having a baby, and looking back at my mother's lifestyle and habits, she, too, must have felt unloved and rejected, not having anyone to turn to for help.

Beforehand, God knew of my parents' traumatic life experiences and met my every need by placing special people and shelters in my life as bridges to where He knew I would need them before I was conceived in my mother's womb. I have forgiven them, letting go of unforgiveness, anger, and pain.

I'm a parent of two young adult children, and parenting is a full-time assignment of choices and decisions. Giving God all the honor and all the praise because He's the one who orchestrated my life story for His purpose, giving me a unique assignment for His glory. I can honestly say, I love my parents.

My father is my hero. Thankfully, he is alive and doing very well. He did the best he knew how with raising a little girl as a Black man in the '70s, just back from the war. I learned from my father how to work, cook, protect, and, most importantly, to love the Lord my God with all my heart, and with all my soul, and with all my mind . . . and to love my neighbor as myself. (Matthew 22:37-39 NIV)

God is an intentional God.

"Before I formed you in the womb I knew you, before you were born I set you apart; I appointed you as a prophet to the nations." (Jeremiah 1:5 NIV)

We were called and chosen to solve a problem. Everything we go through in this journey called life will make us stronger. God knows everything, every strand of hair on our head. We are uniquely designed by Him. He knows every step of our lives. Nothing we have done or are going to do is a shock to God, just to us.

"The thief comes only to steal and kill and destroy; I have come that they may have life, and have it to the full." (John 10:10 NIV)

As you look back over your life, your journeys and pathways may be somewhat similar to mine. Some people start out with a rough life, and some finish rough, but at the end of the day, we all have a story to tell for the Glory of God, and how He was there the whole time. God will always be there to bring us out with victory so that we can help other people in the Kingdom of God. As believers of Jesus Christ, we either win or we learn!

I pray this book blesses you to trust God's plan for your life. You have been called and you have been chosen to solve a problem and to help others. I emphasized that your pain has purpose.

This book will help generations battling with...

1. Anyone who has been raised in a military household.

2. Anyone who's a victim of or has experienced PTSD (post-traumatic stress disorder), triggers, anger, bipolar mood swings,

difficulty processing their emotions, flashbacks, rage, or any other terrifying events that can lead to mental illness behaviors.

3. Anyone who struggles with unforgiveness. (Forgive! Forgiveness is for you, not them.)

4. Anyone who is scarred from living in fear as a child.

5. Anyone who lives in disappointment.

6. Anyone who struggles with failure.

7. Anyone who is dealing with abandonment issues.

8. Anyone who is a single mother.

9. Anyone who is a step-parent or "bonus" parent.

10. Anyone who is being raised in the system (group homes, detention centers, trade schools, or foster homes).

11. Anyone who doesn't know what real love feels like (you will when you find the love of God).

12. Anyone who is living in an abusive home.

13. Anyone who is a "Runaway."

14. Anyone who is an eighth-grade dropout.

15. Those with no education.

16. Anyone who is the "black sheep" of the family.

17. Those with no one to invest in your heart.

18. Anyone craving love and affection.

> *Know that what the enemy meant for evil, God turned it around for my good according to Genesis 50:20 NIV.*

ABOUT THE AUTHOR

Robbin was born into a generation of women who were on welfare and public assistance. They were mishandled, abused, rejected, broken, addicted, poor, and uneducated. However, she overcame it all by discovering herself through her relationship with God. Robbin's favorite bible verse is Philippians 4:13 NKJV, "I can do all things through Christ who strengthens me."

By standing on that verse, Robbin was blessed to start a children's preschool named The Nest in September 2011. She hosts a podcast, *I Am the Body of Christ L.L.C.* (www.iamthebodyofchristpodcast.com), to help encourage, uplift, and spread hope to the world. Despite the hardship she faced as a child, she's determined to break every generational curse in her family.